See Jane Not Run

Teachers Are Leaders

A Family Systems Approach
to
Leadership
for
the Classroom Teacher

Gwen S. Simmons, Ed.D.
Lynda L. Tamblyn, M.Ed.

Cut Above Books
Published by Second Wind Publishing, LLC.
Kernersville

Cut Above Books
Second Wind Publishing, LLC
931-B South Main Street, Box 145
Kernersville, NC 27284

Cut Above Books edition published March, 2009.
Cut Above Books, Running Angel, and all production design are
trademarks of Second Wind Publishing, used under license.

For information regarding bulk purchases of this book, digital
purchase and special discounts, please contact the publisher at
www.secondwindpublishing.com

Cover design by Gwen S. Simmons, Ed.D. and
Lynda L. Tamblyn, M.Ed.

Manufactured in the United States of America

ISBN 978-1-935171-30-0

Visit us at

www.teachersareleaders.com

Acknowledgments

We are indebted to Mike Simpson. He is the teacher who led us to the premise upon which this book is based. He has graciously and generously shared his time, talents, and wisdom in contributing to our lives and to this book. Mike's sense of humor and his encouragement have kept us on track with family systems and with the writing process.

Two groups of educators have been especially helpful in "field testing" the applicability of family systems theory to teachers in the classroom. We thank the leaders and faculties of Ben Martin Elementary School in Fayetteville, North Carolina, and Saint Gertrude High School in Richmond, Virginia.

Gwen Simmons , Ed.D.
Lynda Tamblyn, M.Ed.

Dedicated to Dr. Annie Webb Blanton,

Founder of The Delta Kappa Gamma
Society International

Contents

Introduction

We know one thing for sure about student achievement. In the final analysis, the most important factor in whether students learn is not class size nor curriculum nor the physical plant but the teacher.

Classroom teachers are well aware of the challenges and obstacles related to student achievement. Many of these concerns become so overwhelming and oppressive that the teacher leaves the classroom.

The premise of this book is that by practicing family systems thinking and behaving, teachers will reduce their own stress and anxieties, realize their leadership potential, and be recognized as teacher leaders.

Family systems is predicated upon the fact that families are emotional units. Groups of people who spend significant time together form themselves into similar emotional systems. The relationships within these emotional units replicate the relationships experienced in our families of origin. We can better understand our positions within these formed families if we reflect on our families of origin and what behaviors we have learned within them.

Teachers are, simultaneously, members of emotional units such as classrooms, faculties, schools, professional organizations, religious groups, and their own families. Their abilities to lead within these systems are determined by their relationships with each group's members. Understanding the principles of family systems thinking helps the individual recognize why and how the group functions. Applying the principles enhances his or her ability to lead within the group.

Politicians, school boards, administrators, government officials, and parents seem to have more to say about educational issues than do teachers. Yet, even laymen will acknowledge that it isn't money, bricks and mortar, tangible resources, or technology that makes schooling effective. Only teachers do that.

It is the person of the teacher, the integrity of the teacher, the integrated knowledge, values, beliefs, and passion of the teacher which make a difference to student learning. All subject matter is filtered through the teacher. The teacher, not the subject matter, makes learning come alive for students. Retention of quality classroom teachers is the key to student achievement.

John F. Kennedy said, "...the course of civilization is a race between catastrophe and education." There are no easy solutions to the decline in teacher retention. Without quality classroom teachers, public education is in jeopardy. This is not about a shortage of teachers but rather classroom teachers choosing not to remain in the classroom. Most education professionals who leave their chosen field do so not because they are unable to perform the jobs for which they were trained, but rather because they have encountered tremendous resistance to the successful completion of their professional tasks. In the authors' home state, data indicates about 40% of beginning teachers are leaving teaching within their first five years in the classroom.

Professionals are rigorously trained in how to accomplish the tasks of their profession. Nurses learn how to administer prescribed health care. Clergy learn how to conduct worship and to lead their congregations. Teachers learn appropriate instructional methodology. Few professional schools, including most colleges of education, teach how to function within emotional systems or deal with individuals within those emotional systems who may purposely or inadvertently attempt to prevent the professionals from doing their jobs.

This book is written for classroom teachers. It is not about pay, class size, work environment, enhanced benefits, nor public relations. It is not about fixing problems nor espousing techniques. It is about operating with intentionality at a more conscious level and offers a framework for seeking answers within oneself. It is about encouraging teachers to teach out of who they are rather than what they know. The title emphasizes the hope that Jane (or Dick) will not run from the teaching profession either by leaving the classroom or losing the passion for teaching. It suggests that when faced with obstacles and challenges a teacher who practices the principles of family systems can stand firm in what he or she believes about teaching and learning and students. The discussions of the guiding principles of family systems within this book are intended to encourage classroom teachers to exert the power they have as the leaders they are.

The authors are not experts in family systems theory, but have come to believe in its validity. Over the past ten years they have observed leaders in systems other than education change and grow in personal confidence and make positive differences in their organizations as they practiced family systems concepts. What follows is the authors' distillation of the theory, processes, and principles of family systems applied to an educational setting.

The goal of thinking family systems is not to change the system but to understand it. Systems thinking is not linear, cause and effect, social science quantitative thinking. It is counterintuitive and challenges the security and safety zones of most of us. It isn't a program or a technique, but rather a perspective which sees the classroom and school as sharing the same kinds of dynamics as a family.

A teacher typically sees himself or herself as a helper, a facilitator, a mentor, anything but a leader. If we listen carefully to the language used when talking leadership and teachers in the same sentence, leadership for teachers is viewed in a different fashion than for leaders of businesses or organizations. Teachers make comments and teach workshops about best practices and curriculum and may call attention to the tougher issues by addressing the elephants in the room such as economics, power, race, and cultural differences but that does not mean they are viewed as or view themselves as leaders.

Classroom teachers have not been encouraged nor provided opportunities to participate in leadership training. Because family systems theory mirrors the experiences of growing up within a family, teachers have a head start in thinking family systems since they have less to unlearn about traditional views of leadership.

Getting Personal

In order to become a doctor or lawyer, or any professional, one must be trained by the ultimate professionals – teachers! All of us can remember the powerful influence of a classroom teacher. In fact, most teachers were so positively influenced by one or more of their teachers that they chose teaching as their profession.

Teachers tend to be self-effacing, care-giving individuals who focus on the welfare of others rather than their own well being. They underestimate their significance to everyone else in the school family. Classroom teachers do not recognize how important, compelling, attractive, and essential they are to students, parents, colleagues, administrators, and support staff. Neither does our society as reflected in its eagerness to lay lack of student achievement at the teachers' feet. Teachers absorb such criticism in silence. Those who criticize teachers the most are drawn to teachers because of their power and strength. By the time you finish this text, the authors hope you will be moving toward a fuller awareness of just how important you are as a teacher and leader.

How Did Things Get So Out of Hand?

Teachers are the last to be consulted and the first to be blamed. Public education reflects a system in regression and is in need of thinking differently about the challenges it is facing. What is happening within public education is similar to what was described in the mid-1970s by Murray Bowen as regression in society:

> ... the problem in society was similar to the emotional problem in the family...when a family is subjected to chronic, sustained anxiety, the family begins to lose contact with its intellectually determined principles and to resort more and more to emotionally determined decisions ... The results of this process are symptoms and eventually regression to a lower level of functioning...the same process is evolving in society...we are in a period of increasing societal anxiety...society responds to this with emotionally determined decisions to allay the anxiety of the moment...this results in more band-aid legislation, which increases the problem; and that cycle keeps repeating, just as the family goes through similar cycles to the state we call emotional illness.[1]

There are a multitude of band-aid approaches aimed at reform within public education including private schooling on public dollars, fewer students in a classroom, merit pay, and charter schools. We tend to throw good money after bad. We rarely abandon programs; we keep them for job protection, political influence, or because the resistance to adding a new program is less than trying to rescind an earlier one. There is plenty of blaming and finger-pointing and a plethora of emotionally-based decisions. School administrators hire consultants, fund more research, and take another survey in efforts to collect more data. The system of public education, like the system of our greater society, is *stuck*. And teachers are caught in the "muddle."

Teachers carry the "anxiety football" for the education system. Applying the guiding principles of family systems theory will help teachers reduce the anxiety within themselves and within the system. Sufficient numbers of teachers thinking and acting on these principles just might revitalize education. At the very least, it would ensure more decisions based on intellect and the interest of students instead of the feelings of others or fear of litigation.

A Little Background

The term *stuck* indicates emotional and intellectual immobility. In a stuck organization there is often lots of activity in the name of problem-solving, but there is no indication of long-term success. Decisions are quick-fix and made in an effort to reduce the anxiety of the moment and return to some measure of comfort and security. The longer a system, large or small, remains stuck the more difficult it is to effect change within that system.

In 1997, while looking for ways to revitalize an organization of women educators, the authors became group facilitators for Dr. Mike Simpson, the founder and director of The Lazarus Project. Dr. Simpson's mission was to revitalize stuck churches by using family systems theory to empower ministers as leaders. The ministers met in retreat with Dr. Simpson for as many as three times each year. Listening, learning, and applying systems concepts convinced the authors that not only were family systems concepts applicable to that educational organization for women but that they were especially applicable to the empowerment of the classroom teacher.

The outcome of that awareness is this book. Its intent is to share some guiding principles based on family systems theory and to encourage classroom teachers to remain in the classroom with their integrity intact. The authors believe that teachers who adopt these tenets as standards for their thinking and behavior will recognize themselves, and be recognized by others, as the powerful leaders they are.

A Little More Background

Dr. Murray Bowen, a psychiatrist, was a keen observer of human behavior and developed several concepts which became known as the Bowen Family Systems Theory. He defined the family as an emotional system, one where individuals spent sufficient time together to establish relationships. Bowen's theory focuses on the entire relationship system in contrast to focusing on the individual. His major published work was *Family Therapy in Clinical Practice* which chronicles the development of his work with family systems.

Dr. Edwin Friedman, a student of Dr. Bowen and a rabbi, applied the family systems theory as a leadership model to leaders in many organizations, especially the clergy. His book *Generation to Generation* details the concepts of family process and how they "bring together in one perspective counseling, administration, officiating, preaching, personal growth, and leadership."[2] A year after Friedman's death in 1996, Dr. Mike Simpson, a student of Friedman, initiated work with clergy and published *The Lazarus Project: How You Can Renew Your Congregation.*

Bowen's and Friedman's concepts vary in nomenclature and number. Regardless of how they are named or how they are delineated, family systems concepts are relational – what happens in one part of the system affects the entire system. The system is greater than the sum of its parts.

The approach to self-leadership presented here is viewed through the lenses of Dr. Mike Simpson and his mentor, Dr. Ed Friedman. The book's bias is Friedman's version of Bowen and Simpson's version of Bowen and Friedman.

Chapter 1

You don't need a title to be a leader.

Finding the MVP³ in You

Much of what you are about to read in this text you already know – but may not know that you know. Teachers are leaders. There is no choice as to whether a teacher will lead, but there is a choice about the effectiveness of that leadership.

Mission, vision, and passion are the topics of much discussion in the business world and in education circles. These three components are necessary to the successful tenure of an effective teacher leader and the longevity of any organization. One must be willing to be fired to be an effective leader. That type of risk is associated with one's integrity which involves one's values and the beliefs out of which comes one's mission and passion.

Teachers intuitively come into the teaching profession with a sense of mission and a passion for teaching. Without these, teachers will not remain in the classroom or they may stay to have a paycheck but never be an effective teacher leader. Effective teacher leaders may not formally articulate their mission nor share their passions openly, although both are integral to who they are. This passion and sense of mission distinguishes them from those who enter teaching simply to have a job. A presence of mission and passion within the teacher determines whether she or he happily remains in the classroom.

Teachers sometimes lose their passion for teaching but remain in the classroom. When that happens, the teacher begins to slowly die. Such teachers count the days until retirement or wish for a change of circumstances but they do nothing to effect change. They might even ridicule a beginning teacher who does bring passion and joy to his or her teaching. Teaching without passion is not enjoyable, not productive, and ultimately kills the spirit of the teacher and his or her chance to be an effective teacher leader.

A teacher leader who has integrity is one who stays in touch with her or his personal mission and passion and is transformed by the work she or he does. The process of teaching with integrity energizes the teacher leader rather than depleting her or his energy. A teacher leader with a sense of mission and passion does not burn out but like the Energizer Bunny just keeps going and going and going. Such teacher leaders anticipate and plan for, rather than dread, the beginning of the school year and every Monday morning.

Equally important but not quite so intuitive is the aspect of vision for the teacher leader. As the nursery rhyme indicates, if you do not know where you are going you will not know when you get there. A destination which is recognized upon arrival involves having a vision. Vision is the end result of doing what you do (mission) with whatever drives you to do it (passion).

Staying in touch with one's mission, vision, and passion is key to the enjoyment of a long-term, satisfying, teaching career. When a teacher no longer enjoys going to school an examination of the three is in order. A teacher lacking a sense of mission, vision, and passion is not transformed by the work she or he does and is a candidate for burnout.

The classroom, the local school, and the school systems are emotional units. They each apply pressure on a teacher leader to distance his or her basic self from the process of teaching and to function apart from his or her passion and mission. When faced with the forces of togetherness, the pull of the majority, it is scary to honor the forces of individuality and stand apart as a self.

Family systems thinking can guide a process for teachers to maintain a clear definition of self within multiple emotional systems. It offers something beyond problem solving. Systems thinking does not tell you what to think but it does tell you the importance of knowing what you think. It emphasizes making decisions based on intellect, not emotion. A core concept of family systems is leadership through differentiation of self while being connected to others. A part of self-differentiation at its highest level is when you know your passion, mission, and vision and use those as filters for your actions within your emotional systems each day.

A Different Way to Lead

Self-leadership is personal. The focus is on your personal behavior, not that of others. Self-leadership is adaptive, experiential learning; to be learned, it must be experienced. It cannot be taught but it can be learned through facing a leadership challenge, modifying your perspective, and adapting that learning to the next challenge.

Self-leadership is about developing inner confidence. It is about making the inner you congruent with the outer you. It is not so much a matter of others trusting you as it is a matter of your trusting yourself.

Family systems theorists and practitioners describe the on-going process of growing and leading a self as the differentiation of self[4] or self-differentiation.[5] Regardless of what the process is called, it is the separation of self from, while remaining in, the emotional system of which you are a part.

Leading self is about evaluating your behaviors and values in relationship to and with others. When a person is able to switch from a focus of leading others to a focus on leading self, his or her credibility as a leader increases.

Classroom teachers practicing leadership through self-differentiation will recognize themselves as the leaders they are. In so doing, classroom teachers will discover for themselves that you do not have to have a leadership title to be a leader.

As each of us knows from growing up in our family, we need both contact with others and space as individuals. The challenge in self-differentiation is to not have too much of either. Think of a continuum with fusion with others (togetherness) on one end and being cut-off from others (isolation) on the opposite end. Differentiation of self is a range of behavior, not a static position on the continuum.

Self-differentiation requires being able to distinguish what you think from what you feel and the ability to make decisions based on intellect, not emotion. This differentiation of self involves knowing and honoring your own boundaries and those of others. It means having the ability to move toward or away from others by conscious choice without cutting yourself off from them or merging yourself with them. It is about having pre-determined principles to guide you rather than letting relationships with others direct you.

The process of differentiating a self is on-going and difficult work. The good news is that small increments in growing a self not defined by others will pay big dividends in every emotional system of which you are a part.

A subjective way of assessing the differentiation of self is to note the presence or absence of the first-person pronoun I in conversation. The greater use of "I" statements suggests that one knows where he or she stands on an issue, what he or she thinks, and how he or she feels. In contrast, a person unable to differentiate self from others tends to make more "you" statements and uses such words as you said, you felt, she did, you caused, which indicate a projection onto or the blaming of another.[6] The tendency to make "you" statements is especially obvious during times of stress when there is an inclination to blame others for whatever negative is being experienced.

What we experienced growing up in our family of origin with our parents and siblings has a great deal to do with the degree of differentiation of self. Chances are good that the relationship challenges you face today as a teacher leader are related in some degree to the relationship challenges experienced in your family. You may have had the experience of going back to visit the family of your childhood and being surprised that your adult behavior changed to behavior based on memories, environment, childhood relationships, and family expectations.

Going back to revisit, physically or in reflection, the family of your childhood is an important component of the work of self-differentiation. Many of us have family secrets and traumas which some family members know and discuss while not sharing that information with others in the family. Most families have relatives who do not speak or visit with one another. In family systems, such extreme distancing of a family member is known as a cut-off. The opposite of being cut-off is being too close; this is known as an enmeshed or fused relationship. Emotional cut-offs and the merging of self with others are equally damaging to one's emotional health. In revisiting family of origin relationships, we have an opportunity to unlearn some earlier learned emotional responses and to create a new bank of emotional memories.

A leader who finds a balance between being too close and being too distant from others while being in connection with everyone in her or his system is described as well-differentiated. A person who cannot find a balance and is either fused with or cut-off from persons within the system is described as a poorly differentiated person (PDP). The poorly differentiated person tends to be relationship driven, with a lack of separation or distinction between thinking or feeling. PDPs set up most circumstances and situations as win/lose dichotomies. These folks over-react emotionally to situations or persons and easily fuse with other PDPs.

You as a teacher leader will benefit if you are proactive rather than reactive when dealing with a poorly differentiated person. It is important to realize that PDPs are possibly the most in need of the guidance of the teacher leader – even though they are highly resistant to that leadership. The secret to dealing with a poorly differentiated person is to stay connected, closely monitor that connection, and manage your own anxiety. Poorly differentiated persons are not to be counted upon for loyalty or constancy.

Leadership through self-differentiation involves thinking differently about leadership. Differentiation of self is a process which is difficult and humbling while at the same time energizing. Since it involves a shift in paradigms and a change in thinking, self-leadership can't be learned by taking classes, reading, or attending workshops. Differentiation of a self, like faith, must be practiced and tested to find out how it works for you. Leadership through differentiation of self is learned while thinking on your feet and managing your personal anxiety in the midst of your role as a teacher leader. It is an ongoing quest.

Some keys to leadership through differentiation of self:

- The self of an individual is nurtured, or not nurtured, within early family relationships.
- Every individual inherits a script of family expectations that influences one's behavior patterns.
- Once family scripts are conscious, it is possible to change them.
- Leadership through differentiation of self involves establishing boundaries between self and others.
- Differentiation of a self requires making a clear distinction between what one thinks and what one feels.

- Differentiation of self is about changing self, not one's circumstances.
- Differentiation of self can be theoretically measured by the amount of emotional distance between individuals, e.g., too little space or too much distance indicates a lower level of differentiation.
- It is helpful to create a diagram of one's family of origin and discuss family traumas, rules, secrets, relationships, and ways of dealing with crisis with family members.
- Leadership through differentiation of self involves consciously moving toward or away from others.
- Working on differentiation of self requires risk-taking and a sense of adventure.

How does the notion of leadership through differentiation of self impact the classroom teacher?
- The only person you can change is yourself.
- You can only change a relationship by changing yourself.
- Your challenge is to remain calm when others are anxious.
- As a teacher, focus more on your functioning than on the functioning of others.
- You will benefit from not taking conflict personally.
- You will be well served to separate cognition from emotion when making decisions.
- You will benefit from having a network of other teachers interested in leadership through differentiation of self.

How can a teacher leader deal effectively with leadership through differentiation of self ?

- Be playful when you can.
- Don't take the self-differentiation process or yourself too seriously.
- Distinguish between having a say and having your way.
- Learn to question and face relationship challenges more calmly and less personally.
- Stay connected to everyone in the system.
- Realize that others in the system "go to school" on how the leader responds to a PDP.
- Accept that relationship challenges are replicated in every system and that changing environments does not make them disappear.
- Remind yourself that avoiding negative situations does not make them go away.
- Remember that every form of resistance to leadership relies to a degree on the complicity of the leader.
- Consider the possibility that your ability as a teacher leader to lead the system is in direct proportion to your willingness to abandon comfort and security.
- Learn to take care of yourself to the extent you take care of others.
- Determine where you stand on an issue and articulate your position.
- Remember when one person in a relationship over-functions, it gives permission to the other to under-function.

- Don't allow personal relationships to get in the way of decisions based on tangible, factual evidence.
- Assume responsibility for your emotional well-being.

Questions for Reflection:
1. Who would suffer if you started taking better care of yourself?
2. Under what circumstances and when did you take a stand on an issue and what were the results?
3. From whom in your personal systems of classroom, school, and family, do you feel too distant? too close?
4. What script of expectations did you receive from your family of origin?
5. In what relationship situations do you feel inferior? superior? equal?
6. What is your best memory of your childhood?
7. In times of crisis, can you separate how you feel from what you think?

Chapter 2

The only person you can change is yourself.

Look for the Triangles

If asked "Who is the most important member of your family?", many parents would answer "Our child." From a family systems perspective, the parents as the recognized leaders of the family are key to the family's functioning and surviving; therefore they are the most valuable to the family.

If asked "Who is the most important person in the classroom?", many teachers would answer "The student." As with the parent in the family, the teacher is the leader in the classroom and as such is its most valuable person. Students expect and want you to lead. You can't make the students learn nor can you change their personal circumstances. The only person whose behavior you really control is your own. If real change is desired, it must begin with changing yourself.

In family systems thinking, a system exists when persons spend sufficient time together to develop relationships. Wherever human beings gather they intuitively form themselves into groups, or emotional systems.

You, your siblings and your parents constitute a system with strong emotional ties. In that framework of relationships you learned to respond to threats or perceived threats to the family unit. Those responses included tendencies to either flee the situation or fight. Emotional responses within families tend to be predictable. The relationship challenges we experience in our adult systems are directly related to the relationship challenges we experienced growing up in our family of origin. Family systems theory validates that what we know about human relationships we learned as we grew up.

The classroom is an emotional system. It has boundaries, has subgroups, and has messages and rules which shape the behavior of it members. The classroom is made up of individual students but the whole unit has an identity, or reputation, all its own. The classroom has a leader and then other leaders within it as members form subgroups.

The dynamics observed in classroom relationships are the same as the emotional dynamics in our families. The actions of one or two affect the class as a unit. We comment about classroom relationship dynamics in the same ways we comment about relationships within our families.

A greater understanding of family systems helps us to accept, and not take personally, most human behaviors. Family systems thinking encourages objective caring and concern for others and an equal caring and concern for self. This approach minimizes the potential for burnout.

The metaphor of a mobile above a baby's crib offers insight into the simplicity of the family process concepts and the complexity of trying to explain them. One touch of the mobile by the baby and all parts are impacted. You can't stop the momentum of the mobile to examine which piece touched what part first. Like the relationships within the mobile, what happens in one part of the system affects the entire system.

The concept of triangles, like the concepts of the well-differentiated leader and connectedness, is basic to systems thinking. Triangles are comprised of two individuals and their relationships to a third person. They are the basic building blocks of human relationships. Two persons cannot talk long before mentioning a third person. A triangle can be positive or negative. The relationships within a triangle are always changing. When relationship difficulties present themselves, look for the triangle and determine your position in it. Certain rules apply to relationship triangles.[7]

Rule 1 - You can only change a relationship to which you belong.

Rule 2 - If you try to change the relationship of the side to which you are not connected, the results usually will be the opposite of what you intend.

Rule 3 - If you break Rule #2, you will end up with little or no satisfaction and more stress and anxiety.

To implement rule 1, maintain a relationship with each of the persons in the triangle and avoid the responsibility for their relationship with one another. To illustrate rule 2 and rule 3, identify the three corners of a triangle as A, B, and C. Mother A has a daughter B who is dating guy C. If mother A tries to push daughter B and guy C apart, the result will often be a closer relationship between B and C and mother A will end up being the stressed one.

Some keys to emotional triangles:

- Triangles are the building blocks of all relationships.
- Triangles are neither good nor bad; they just are.
- Triangles cannot be avoided.
- Triangles form when two people get uncomfortable with their relationship and bring in a third party.
- Triangles are extremely malleable and potential for change is constant.
- Secrets and gossip are often a part of triangle formation.
- Triangles are emotional constructs which add enough stability to our lives to enable us to function effectively.
- If one or more persons from one triangle join another triangle, there is greater potential for creating an us against them mentality.
- A triangle can be changed when one person changes his or her behavior.
- We can examine our relationships and the triangles in which those relationships exist and posit whether they are nurturing or toxic to us.
- Triangles transmit a system's stress to its most responsible or most focused member.

How does the notion of emotional triangles impact the classroom teacher?

- How you relate within and to triangles determines who gets to carry the anxiety.
- As a teacher, your best relationship to most classroom triangles is as an outsider.

- Understanding your position in a triangle will guide your decision to move toward or away from the individuals in the triangle.
- You have the potential to exit, create, or reform a triangle in order to move it to a more positive state.

How can the teacher leader deal effectively with emotional triangles ?

- Objectively examine the triangles in which the level of anxiety is high and ask questions instead of offering solutions.
- Utilize your knowledge of triangles as a leadership tool.
- Resist your natural tendency to avoid persons with whom you disagree.
- Remember that triangles are created in an effort to reduce the discomfort and increase the stability within relationships.
- Memorize the three rules of triangles and apply them when facing relationship challenges.

Questions for reflection:

1. Are the triangles in your family of origin easy to identify?
2. Can you envision a positive triangle situation that involves a parent, teacher, and principal?
3. When did an effort on your part to fix a relationship between two people backfire?
4. How do you feel when you move toward or away from a person in a triangle relationship?

Chapter 3

Cut them off at the cut-off.

Fused, Cut-off, or Connected?

A style of leadership arising from the perspective of family systems is leadership by a well-differentiated person who leads through connection. The goal of connectedness is to achieve differentiation of self to the degree that one is not fused with (too close to) nor cut off from (too distant from) other individuals within the system. It is about retaining one's integrity while staying connected to others, not merging with or separating from anyone. An ideal relationship is open and honest with separate, but equal, partners.

Let's face it. There are people with whom we simply do not want to be connected. A significant aspect of connectedness for the teacher leader is his or her willingness to be connected to those with whom connection is distasteful. Connectedness can be achieved without sacrificing position, vision or authority. In family systems thinking, connectedness is a most important aspect of a system's vitality and, by extension, the effectiveness of its leader depends on his or her ability to maintain connectedness.

To be connected implies a comfortable level of non-anxious contact with everyone in the system. It does not imply feeling close; it is not necessary to like or love someone to be connected. You can have an emotional connection with little or no physical contact because of geographical distance or you can be physically in the same room without emotional connection.

What is required to be a teacher leader who leads by connection? It requires working to maintain a self-differentiated relationship with each person in the system and remembering that the classroom is, as is any system, always in flux. Within any system certain members are unwilling or unable to regulate themselves and are much more likely to require a leader's time and attention. Certain students will set the tenor of the classroom and demand the teacher's time and attention unless limits are set for those students. The ability to maintain a well-connected and non-anxious classroom presence seems to breed the same types of relationship with one's peers and superiors. The need to remain connected relates to the age-old saying, " Keep your friends close and your enemies closer."

As a classroom teacher, you face various forms of resistance to your leadership every day. There are four basic forms of resistance: when the forces of resistance are obvious to you (attack), when the resistance comes from folks you thought were friends (sabotage), when the system itself seems to swallow you with its concerns that are irrelevant to your mission and vision (fusion), and when the resistance is expressed by distancing from you (cut-off).

Attack, sabotage, and fusion as forms of resistance are easily recognized. Cut-off, on the other hand, is not as obvious. Being cut off is the opposite of being connected; it describes a relationship out of emotional balance. When two people are cut off, the emotional discomfort interferes with communication and productivity.

Some keys to connectedness:

- Family systems is about leadership by being connected to everyone in the system.
- Connectedness requires the ability and the willingness to move toward or away from others.
- Connectedness requires constant attention and continual work.
- Trauma or crisis in a system heightens the likelihood of disconnection or a cut-off.
- Every system has cut-offs.
- Cut-offs exist on a continuum from a total breaking of communication to cordial aloofness and unspoken, unaddressed emotional distance.
- Cut-offs may be handed-down from generation to generation.
- Cut-offs are an attempt to avoid pain, honesty and self-examination and the anxiety that accompanies them.
- Cut-offs imply some type of secret and secrets imply some type of cut-off.
- Cut-offs can be healed, but do not heal of their own accord.
- Connectedness promotes healing by diminishing anxiety.

How does the notion of connectedness impact the classroom teacher?

- Your ability to remain connected is the single greatest test of your effectiveness as a teacher.

- You are a part of multiple, interlocking systems.
- Your ability to be playful with others indicates connection.
- Disconnection, or emotional distance, can alter your vision and mission as a teacher.
- You can expect persons within the systems to which you belong to have unresolved emotional issues (cut-offs) which will be projected onto you.

How can a teacher leader deal effectively with connectedness?

- Choose to stay connected to everyone in the system.
- Don't disconnect (cut off) from attackers.
- Identify and discuss cut-offs within your family of origin.
- Practice emotionally moving toward or away from others.
- Remember that connectedness is typically initiated by the leader of the system.
- Remember that the emotional dynamics of connectedness are the same regardless of the positions held within the system.
- Reassure yourself that maintaining connectedness becomes less difficult with practice.
- Anticipate resistance and choose to remain focused on one's goals, mission, and vision.
- Learn to put your welfare first.
- Choose to be playful and non-anxious when others are overly serious.

- Remember that you will not be able to maintain a non-anxious presence and a willingness to be connected all of the time.
- Recognize that working through healing a cut-off in a system may have a corollary, positive effect on other members of that system and on other systems of which you are a part.
- Be aware that attacks are in actuality troubled bids by the attacker to achieve connectedness with you, the teacher leader.

Questions for reflection:
1. What are some ways you have tried to re-connect to persons in your life who previously have been cut-off?
2. How were negative events or crisis situations handled in your family of origin?
3. Who knew your family secrets and talked about them with certain members of the family but not with others?
4. What in your childhood do you remember about talking to or not talking to certain relatives?
5. Who in your family makes attempts to stay connected to everyone in the family?

Chapter 4

Hand off the anxiety football.

Be a Non-Anxious Presence

Teachers tend to be the symptom bearers of what is broken in education. It is easier to displace anxiety onto a symptom bearer in a system than it is to examine the effectiveness of a system's leadership. A system will transmit its stress to the most responsible or focused member. Because teachers care about students and their learning, they tend to assume the most responsibility for making learning happen. In addition to assuming responsibility for quality teaching and facilitation of students' learning, others expect and teachers often assume responsibility for the learning outcome as well. Awareness of family process within the education system will allow teachers to hand back the system's anxiety and find their voices to speak with authority about what is best for students. When teachers begin to perceive themselves as leaders they will focus on leading, rather than being led.

The challenge is to be non-anxious and present in the midst of anxiety. The degree to which you can be a non-anxious presence determines your effectiveness as a leader. The keys to being non-anxious are staying connected to everyone in the system, knowing and stating your mission and vision, and being undeterred by any resistance you face.

Anxiety is negative energy. A degree of anxiety helps us be motivated and moves us forward toward our goals. Excessive anxiety can immobilize us and make rational thinking more difficult. Anxiety is contagious and spreads easily and quickly through a system. Solicitous concern and uneasiness of mind are two defining characteristics of anxiety. The carrier of the anxiety earnestly wishes for circumstances to be different.

Anxiety may be either chronic or acute. Acute anxiety is the fearfulness that pervades a system as a result of a current trauma or situation. If a key leader of the system were to become terminally ill or the treasurer absconds with the organization's financial reserves, the anxiety of the group would be acute. Chronic anxiety, on the other hand, is constant and represents an underlying fearfulness that pervades a system. Irrational resistance to risk taking, flexibility, and creativity indicates the presence of a system's chronic anxiety.

We cope with acute and chronic anxiety in various ways. Conflict or attack, distancing or cutting-off, forming triangles, and over-functioning or under-functioning are our attempts to minimize anxiety. Of these, classroom teachers often turn to over-functioning behaviors to manage this anxiety.

> One of the most universal complaints from clergy of all faiths is the feeling of being stuck with all the responsibility. ... It is never possible to make others responsible by trying to make them responsible, because the very act of trying to make others responsible is preempting their responsibility. ... Overfunctioning in any system is an anxious response in both

senses of the word 'anxious' as in anticipatory and 'anxious' as in fearful. ...One of the subtlest yet most fundamental effects of overfunctioning is spiritual. It destroys the spiritual quality of the overfunctioner. 8

Although Friedman was speaking specifically about clergy what he says about over-functioning holds true for leaders of any system, especially teacher leaders. Over-functioning is doing for another what he or she can do for himself or herself. The only way to teach responsibility is to delegate it and not take it back. If one person in a relationship over-functions, the other person under-functions. In any partnership the more anxious a partner is to accomplish a task, the less motivated the other partner will be to take responsibility. Classroom teachers, with urging from inside and outside the system, tend to over-function and carry the system's anxiety.

A teacher's over-functioning leads to loss of passion for teaching and to burn-out. When this happens, the teacher leaves the profession, either physically or emotionally.

Some keys to anxiety:

- The person who is best able to maintain a non-anxious connectedness to everyone in the system has the best chance of being accepted as the leader.
- A negative result of heightened anxiety is a diminished ability to recognize alternatives.
- Anxiety reduces the system's and the leader's ability to see the big picture.
- Anxiety is highly contagious.
- Crises tend to resolve themselves over a period of time.
- Polarization in a system reveals chronic anxiety.

35

- The degree of chronic anxiety is lessened when the system's leader has neither a too distant nor too close relationships with members of the system.
- Systems, like human beings, have immune systems.
- Immune systems can only endure a certain degree of anxiety.

How does the notion of anxiety impact the classroom teacher?
- The tendency to over-function or under-function in relationships is inversely related to your ability to maintain a non-anxious presence.
- You can develop the demeanor of a non-anxious leader.
- Carrying others' anxiety reduces your vitality and strength and ultimately leads to burnout.
- Your ability to be connected and maintain a non-anxious presence with a superior will lead to an increased ability to do the same in the classroom.

How can a teacher leader deal effectively with anxiety?
- Discover options to catching and carrying the system's anxiety.
- Remind yourself that the antidote to anxiety in a system is connectedness.
- Remind yourself that a crisis does not last forever.
- Get less anxious if your goal is to lessen the anxiety of others.
- Remember that how you deal with anxiety determines the level of anxiety within the system.
- Resist becoming defensive when sabotaged or attacked and invest your energy in working to stay connected.

- Remember that others can control you if they know you better than you know yourself.
- Be aware of and work on your own issues to avoid having your hot buttons pushed by the more dependent members in the system.
- Know the difference between handing off anxiety and shirking authority.

Questions for reflection:
1. How was anxiety managed when a crisis or trauma occurred in your family of origin? Did anyone get extremely quiet or loud? Did they hug or distance themselves? Did family members take sides?
2. Who was the peacemaker in your family when you were growing up?
3. How would you describe the emotional atmosphere in your family of origin? In your grandparents' home? What stories are re-told at each family reunion?
4. What do you do to de-stress yourself?
5. What is your pattern of behavior in dealing with conflict?

Chapter 5

If I'm frowning, I must be important.

Misery Loves Company

Anxiety invariably presents itself as seriousness. Just as misery loves company, so seriousness and anxiety have a need for converts. Seriousness within a system, though often mistaken for significance or importance, is a way of saying to the leader, "You don't seem to realize that this is something you should be worried about."

The opposite of seriousness is playfulness, an attitude of joyfulness and spontaneity. Playfulness has no need for converts, and in fact, calls more attention to itself when it emerges in the midst of an anxious group. Playfulness, particularly in the face of abject seriousness, is a way of saying that one will not be trapped by the contagious nature of seriousness nor fall for attempts at manipulation by the serious one. The most attractive part of interpersonal relationships is playfulness. Relationships which last the longest and are the most vital continue to have pronounced elements of playfulness.

Playfulness is a desired behavior for a teacher leader. Playfulness, like other leadership skills, requires patience and practice to use effectively. Playfulness is not forced. Playfulness transcends the ability to tell stories resulting in peals of laughter. Playfulness implies an attitude of joyfulness to a greater extent than it implies funniness. Do not expect playfulness to be universally blessed. When one does something that is inappropriate to the moment – and that is what humor is– time and thought are often required for others present to catch up. Each person possesses a unique sense of humor. Trust yours.

Being playful and pretending to be playful are not the same. There are times when one cannot be playful. Trying to be playful or humorous when feeling angry or indignant risks coming across as being mean. Forced playfulness, especially in an anxious situation, can sound sarcastic and cynical. There are those who pretend to be playful who are in fact cutting and highly manipulative.

Seriousness, as with all forms of anxiety, tends to create division and destroy functional emotional connectedness. Playfulness, on the other hand, promotes connectedness by moving toward an individual or a group and implies that a creative emotional distance is being maintained. It is a non-threatening invitation for others to move toward the playful one with the promise that good things will result.

Where there is a void of playfulness, there is an inability to be spontaneous. The facial expressions of the overly serious are typically pained and unpleasant. It is characteristic of those adults who seek to control an entire system to be serious. Chronically serious people assume authority they do not possess and attempt to control with their seriousness.

Some keys to seriousness and playfulness :
- Seriousness is a form of manipulation.
- The loss of playfulness is an indication of emotional immaturity.
- Overly serious people tend to emotionally blackmail others.
- Chronically serious persons control by disapproving

and actively delaying what otherwise would be quickly accomplished.

- Seriousness is a form of freezing a relationship at a certain emotional distance.
- Seriousness implies an unequal relationship, i.e., the authority of the serious one and the dependence on the part of the other.
- Seriousness implies that bad things will happen if there is no capitulation to the serious one.
- Intimacy, which requires the ability to get closer than is ordinarily acceptable, is not possible with those who are chronically serious.
- The antidote to seriousness is playfulness.

How does the notion of seriousness and playfulness impact the classroom teacher?

- Being playful is one way for you to achieve connectedness.
- Remembering that seriousness is a major tool of dis-empowerment will help you avoid manipulation by a chronically serious colleague.
- You will benefit from challenging the supposition that one who expresses seriousness is focused upon something more important than is one who is not so serious.
- When you use playfulness as an antidote to anxiety and seriousness you will encourage more playfulness in others.
- A chronically serious environment or instructional leader robs you of your creativity, joyfulness, energy, and willingness to take risks.

How can a teacher leader deal effectively with seriousness and playfulness?

- Learn to be playful.
- Trust your sense of humor.
- View playfulness as a barometer of the anxiety in a system and the effectiveness of its leader.
- Use playfulness to prevent chronically serious individuals from defining the system, the leader, or the task at hand in serious terms.
- Refuse to become overly anxious with a chronically anxious colleague by using your tone of voice, words, and body language to say, "I am not disregarding this, but I am not taking it too seriously."
- Ask questions rather than making statements in response to the chronically serious person's arguments and complaints.
- Be with children, young people, and playful adults on a regular basis.
- Earn a reputation as being a playful person.

Questions for reflection:

1. Rate the playfulness in your classroom on a scale of one to ten, with one being a root canal and ten being a litter of puppies.
2. Name the most playful leader you've known. How did he or she react in a crisis?
3. How long has it been since you had a real belly laugh? What were the circumstances?
4. Who in your school is most immune to seriousness?
5. How do the serious folks in your school cope with the playful ones?

6. How can you be playful within your natural sense of humor?
7. Who was the most playful person in your family of origin?
8. Where do you go and what do you do to lighten up?

Chapter 6

No good deed goes unpunished.

A Teacher Leader Can Be Anything But a Sissy

As a teacher leader, expect criticism and conflict. Criticism usually has an element of truth in it but when criticism is irrational and without any substance it is a form of pursuit. Chances are you have noted that identified issues expressed as criticism are rarely the real problem. Criticism has two basic elements, content and process.

The underlying emotional reality is the process. Content is the verbalized reason for the criticism. Recognizing the difference between content and process helps evaluate the validity of the criticism and understand the motivation of the critic.

Content is the small talk people make when they are infatuated with each other. Process is the emotional magnetism which draws them together. "Content is the stuff people argue about; process is the reason they argue."[9]

Although rarely the real issue in criticism or complaints, content is not to be ignored. There is a tendency to disregard content once we have realized it is unsubstantiated. While ultimately the river (process) is far more consequential than the junk (content) floating on it, driftwood caught up in white-water can kill you if it hits you in the head. Absurd and seemingly insignificant issues should be acknowledged.

An important distinction to make in negotiating the river of emotional process is the difference between feelings and emotions. Feelings are within our awareness.

Emotions are powerful automatic states that are often unconscious. Feelings are transitory. Emotional process is constant. For example, when a child belches at the dinner table the reaction may vary depending on what mood we're in or who is eating with us. If we see that same child fall out of a tree and lie motionless on the ground, the emotional response would be the same regardless of the mood we are in or who is with us.[10]

Emotional process reflects the deepest of human emotions. It is powerful and explosive and is to be dealt with cautiously. Ultimately, blowing a kiss to the content[11] or accepting that kernel of truth in the criticism opens doors through which one has access to the more significant and underlying issues of emotional process. Even when a great deal of trust is present, individuals will distance themselves when process issues are mentioned. The right to openly approach emotional process in people's lives is earned, not assumed.

The next time someone verbally attacks you, remember the two components of criticism and evaluate both content and process before making any response. Resist becoming defensive and think about the possibility that the critic wants or needs something from you.

Some keys to criticism:
- Emotional process is neither negative nor positive; it just is.
- Depending on the circumstances, emotional process may be experienced as pleasant or unpleasant, as beneficial or detrimental, or as healing or destructive.
- An effective leader is attractive and compelling to persons within that system.

- Followers in any system tend to pursue the leader of the system in proportion to their own needs.
- Criticism may be a form of pursuit.[12]
- When things are going extremely well, watch out.
- A logical defense is ineffective in responding to criticism based on emotional process.
- When someone attacks a leader, most of the time the presenting issue is not the real, underlying issue.
- The more anxious and emotional an attacker is, the greater the chances that the issue is emotional and not content.
- In life as in the river metaphor, it is much easier to focus on what is floating in the river, the content, than to focus on the river, the emotional process, itself.

How does the notion of criticism impact the classroom teacher?

- Criticism is to be expected and does not disqualify you as a leader.
- Separating content and process within criticism will diminish your anxiety.
- The most pernicious obstacles you face are not attacks on your strengths but rather on your weaknesses.
- Criticism increases your anxiety, can throw you off balance, and may deter your efforts.
- You lead by the position you hold in the system and your emotional connection to everyone.

How can a teacher leader deal effectively with criticism?

- Use more questions than declarative statements when responding to criticism.

- Remind yourself that gossip and unjustified complaints are forms of pursuit.
- Remind yourself that criticism indicates a degree of admiration by your critic.
- Remember that the important questions in the face of criticism are "How can I stay connected when I would really like to disconnect?" and "What does this person want from me?"
- Be aware that your best compliments may be the ones that irritate you the most.
- Avoid reacting impetuously or spontaneously to criticism.
- Work to stay connected to the critic from whom you would really like to disconnect.
- Give yourself enough time to calm down after being attacked or sabotaged before you talk about the situation with anyone.
- Wait until you have calmed down after a major blow-up and think of a genuinely playful and non-threatening way to re-establish connection with your critic.
- Control your own anxiety in the face of criticism.
- Remind yourself that, in general, the less anxious the leader is about the critic the less trouble the critic can cause.
- Treat your critics with grace and dignity by not cutting them off.
- React in a non-anxious, non-defensive manner when facing criticism.
- Remember that a crisis cannot be solved, only managed.

- Recognize that people who make more "you" statements than "I" statements are in a blaming mode and are not well-differentiated.

Questions for reflection:

1. What messages did you learn about criticism in your family of origin?
2. What are your weaknesses? What are your strengths?
3. What happened when you were criticized as a child? Who came to your rescue? What did you do?
4. What happened when you criticized someone in your family or neighborhood?
5. Can you think of a time when you traded your personal beliefs for the sake of approval?
6. In what ways could the concept that criticism is a form of pursuit be useful?

Chapter 7

Enjoy the adventure.

Don't take yourself too seriously.

"Nobody gets this stuff right 100% of the time. ... The best we can hope for is seven days out of ten."[13] This 70% rule is full of grace. It assures us that our efforts are worthwhile even though we fall short of perfection.

Don't let someone dip from your bucket unless it is full.

Take care of you. Avoid assuming responsibility for the functioning of others. That position is most dangerous to your health. Giving up self in the interest of togetherness guarantees that you carry the anxiety for the entire system. Evidence supports that "there is a powerful relationship between good physical health ... on one hand, and differentiation of self, on the other."[14]

Assess where you are, decide where you want to be, and move in that direction.

Step back. Look at yourself from a systems point of view.

What are the issues?
What do you think?
What do you feel?

Are you satisfied with your behaviors?
How would you like things to be different?
Where do you want to be?

What is the first step in getting there?
Who or what can be of help?
What are your resources?

Your impact is endless.
Determine your guiding principles.
Maintain your integrity.
Realize your value.
Focus on your mission.
Find your voice.
Teach with passion.

Following family process requires a sense of adventure. Use your intellectually determined principles to recalculate your emotional guidance system if you take a wrong turn. Begin the journey. Travel one moment, one minute, one day at a time. *The real voyage of discovery consists not of finding new lands but of seeing the territory with new eyes.* – Marcel Proust

Notes

The numbers referenced in this text refer to:

Blackwell, M.C., *Upside Down Leadership: a Dozen Big Ideas to Turn Your Nonprofit Organization Right Side Up*, Parkway Publishers, Inc., Boone NC, 2003. Use of MVP acronym by permission of the author.

Bowen, Murray, *Family Therapy in Clinical Practice*, Rowman & Littlefield Publishers, Inc., Lanham MD, 1985. (First published 1978)

Friedman, Edwin, *Generation to Generation*, The Guilford Press, New York NY, 1985.

Simpson, Mike, *The Lazarus Project: How You Can Renew Your Congregation*, 2nd Wind Press, Greensboro NC, 1999.

Simpson, Mike, Presentations at The Lazarus Project in retreat, 1997-2007. Used with permission of the author.

1. Bowen, p. 386

2. Friedman, p. 2

3. Blackwell

4. Bowen, p. 467

5. Friedman, p.228

6. Friedman, p. 27

7. Friedman, p. 36-39

8. Friedman, p. 211-212

9. Simpson, p. 85

10. Simpson, presentation

11. Simpson, presentation

12. Friedman, p. 264

13. Simpson, p. 88-89

14. Friedman, p. 135

Addendum

Mission and Vision and Passion

Some keys to mission, vision, and passion :
- A mission explains the reason for doing what one does.
- An articulated vision defines a future outcome of one's mission; it describes what or who one wants to become.
- Neither a mission or vision is achievable without passion.
- Without passion a teacher leader is a spectator, not a participant, in the learning process.
- Passion is the personal, inner fire which drives mission and vision.
- A teacher leader who is clear about her or his personal values and beliefs will have a mission, vision, and passion related to those values and beliefs.
- A teacher leader with a mission, vision, and passion will find and use his or her public voice on educational issues.
- If the teacher leader is not clear about the functions of her or his position, the job's description will be decided for her or him.

Thoughts on formalizing a mission as a teacher leader and writing a mission statement:
- Developing a mission statement is a process and that requires time for reflection; it is not a process to be hurried.

- One's mission should answer the question, "What am I doing now?", e.g., the mission of the Red Cross is "to serve the most vulnerable."
- A mission statement should be succinct, easy to memorize and recite.
- Be succinct when writing a mission statement; cut the number of words in half and then cut them in half again.
- A mission statement should be clear and easily understood.
- One's mission should act as a filter for one's behavior and actions.

Thoughts on formalizing your vision as a teacher leader and writing a vision statement:
- Formalizing a vision statement allows one to forecast the end result of one's mission.
- A vision statement records what or who one wants to become.
- A vision statement is important to seeing and articulating possibilities.
- One cannot go where one cannot visualize.

Thoughts on the importance of passion to the teacher leader and its relationship to mission and vision:
- Passion precedes a teacher's sense of mission and vision.
- Passion determines the teacher leader's mission and shapes her or his vision.
- Passion indicates a teacher's values and beliefs.

- Passion, in and of itself, is hard to describe but its presence or absence is easily recognized.
- Teachers may be passionate about many things but a certain passion brought them into teaching.
- Most teacher leaders have a passion related to improving the human condition, especially that of their students.
- Teacher leaders are passionate about continuing to learn and being more effective presenters of their disciplines' content.

About the Authors

The authors are retired educators with extensive backgrounds in coaching, Gwen as a counselor and life coach and Lynda as teacher and high school athletics coach. They live and work in North Carolina.

They served as facilitators for Mike Simpson's Lazarus Project retreats from 1997-2007. During that time they came to view leadership through the family systems approach as a key to the effectiveness of the classroom teacher and to the retention of quality teachers.

An ongoing series of serendipitous events has nudged, then pushed, them towards the creation of this book.

Gwen S. Simmons, Ed.D.
- Retired Director of the Counseling and Testing Center, University of North Carolina at Pembroke, Pembroke, NC
- Twenty-eight years teaching and counseling in North Carolina education systems; Licensed Professional Counselor, Licensed Clinical Addictions Specialist
- Member of The Delta Kappa Gamma Society International since 1979

Lynda L. Tamblyn, M.Ed.
- Retired Chairman of the Physical Education Department, Grimsley High School, Greensboro, NC
- Thirty years teaching and coaching in North Carolina public schools
- Member of The Delta Kappa Gamma Society International since 1981

Made in the USA